SHARING; JOY, LIBERTY

VOLUME 1: PRECEPTS

ADRIAN B EARLY

ACKNOWLEDGEMENTS

It is impossible to mention all who contributed through my life, culminating in this sharing system and book. It would be required to include them all to do justice to a statement like this. But, I here mention my parents, John O Early and Martha S Early, who I love and miss greatly, my dear sweet devoted Kathy, who died from cancer, and my wonderful sweetheart, Mary. These especially helped me grow, love, and care.

I greatly appreciate everyone who contributed to StockRoller, through arduous layering of value, dealing with regulatory issues, etc., especially Pastor Michael Peschke, who is not required to help, but cares deeply, and Brady Otts. Thank you, Shawn Hallman. Nuanced editing of yours improved the book markedly. It would be less, and published later, without your dedication to the ideals of StockRoller, this work, and its completion.

I am very grateful for the encouragement and guidance in this work from Dr. Norman Horn, Founder of Christians For Liberty, Alexander McCobin, Founder of Students For Liberty, my good friend Peter Reardon, Reverend Lance Richards, Reverend Wanda Bess, Dr. Don House, and Professor Kenda Creasy Dean.

CONTENTS

PREFACE

From early childhood I have been fascinated by understanding how the world works. This includes not only physical phenomena, what we call science, but also how people work; what drives them, how they behave and why, both as individuals and in groups. And related to both head and heart based drivers of behavior.

Early in the new millennium, marked perhaps coincidentally (or not) with 9/11/2001, during the first residence week kicking off my Executive MBA program, I became increasingly concerned about how society seemed to not be working for people. I felt we had delegated to others what close knit communities had long done for their members; caring for needs, especially in times of adversity. It seemed the result was that fewer actually cared themselves.

I believed my knowledge and interest in engineering, economics, finance and investing, and insights from scripture might point the way to a market based, voluntary solution to the demands for economic "correction" of inequality in outcome. The gleaning Ruth did in the fields of Boaz seemed to emerge as a model. This book outlines that "technology", modernized to the new era of capital.

INTRODUCTION

This Pickle Jar story[i] circulated by email:

The pickle jar as far back as I can remember sat on the floor beside the dresser in my parents' bedroom. When he got ready for bed, Dad would empty his pockets and toss his coins into the jar.

As a small boy I was always fascinated at the sounds the coins made as they were dropped into the jar. They ended with a merry jingle when the jar was almost empty. Then the tones gradually muted to a dull thud as the jar was filled. I used to squat on the floor in front of the jar and admire the copper and silver circles that glinted like a pirate's treasure when the sun poured through the bedroom window.

When the jar was filled, Dad would sit at the kitchen table and roll the coins before taking them to the bank. Taking the coins to the bank was always a big production. Stacked neatly in a small cardboard box, the coins were placed between Dad and me on the seat of his old truck. Each and every time, as we drove to the bank, Dad would look at me hopefully. "Those coins are going to keep you out of the textile mill, son.

You're going to do better than me. This old mill town's not going to hold you back." Also, each and every time, as he slid the box of rolled coins across the counter at the bank toward the cashier, he would grin proudly.

"These are for my son's college fund. He'll never work at the mill all his life like me." We would always celebrate each deposit by stopping for an ice cream cone. I always got chocolate. Dad always got vanilla. When the clerk at the ice cream parlor handed Dad his change, he would show me the few coins nestled in his palm. "When we get home, we'll start filling the jar again."

He always let me drop the first coins into the empty jar. As they rattled around with a brief, happy jingle, we grinned at each other. "You'll get to college on pennies, nickels, dimes and quarters," he said. "But you'll get there. I'll see to that."

The years passed, and I finished college and took a job in another town. Once, while visiting my parents, I used the phone in their bedroom, and noticed that the pickle jar was gone. It had served its purpose and had been removed. A lump rose in my throat as I stared at the spot beside the dresser where the jar had always stood. My dad was a man of few words, and never lectured me on the values of determination, perseverance, and faith. The pickle jar had taught me all these virtues far more eloquently than the most flowery of words could have done.

When I married, I told my wife Susan about the significant part the lowly pickle jar had played in my life as a boy. In my mind, it defined, more than anything else, how much my dad had loved me. No matter how rough things got at home, Dad continued to doggedly drop his coins into the jar. Even the summer when Dad got laid off from the mill, and Mama had to serve dried beans several times a week, not a single dime was taken from the jar.

To the contrary, as Dad looked across the table at me, pouring catsup over my beans to make them more palatable, he became more determined than ever to make away out for me. "When you finish college, Son," he told me, his eyes glistening, "You'll never have to eat beans again...unless you want to."

The first Christmas after our daughter Jessica was born, we spent the holiday with my parents. After dinner, Mom and Dad sat next to each other on the sofa, taking turns cuddling their first grandchild. Jessica began to whimper softly, and Susan took her from Dad's arms. "She probably needs to be changed," she said, carrying the baby into my parents' bedroom to diaper her. When Susan came back into the living room, there was a strange mist in her eyes. She handed Jessica back to Dad before taking my hand and leading me into the room.

"Look," she said softly, her eyes directing me to a spot on the floor beside the dresser. To my amazement, there, as if it had never been removed, stood the old pickle jar, the bottom already covered with coins. I walked over to the pickle jar, dug down into my pocket, and pulled out a fistful of coins.

With a gamut of emotions choking me, I dropped the coins into the jar. I looked up and saw that Dad, carrying Jessica, had slipped quietly into the room. Our eyes locked, and I knew he was feeling the same emotions I felt. Neither one of us could speak.

– Author Unknown

Sharing is a network or community doing this systematically, for all participants, regardless of the need, or opportunity, or when it may be required.

Chapter 1
God's Public Policy

When you reap the harvest of your land, do not reap to the very edges of your field or gather the gleanings of your harvest. Do not go over your vineyard a second time or pick up the grapes that have fallen. Leave them for the poor and the foreigner. I am the Lord your God.

- Leviticus 19: 9 and 10 (New International Version)

Now Naomi had a relative on her husband's side, a man of standing from the clan of Elimelek, whose name was Boaz. And Ruth the Moabite said to Naomi, "Let me go to the fields and pick up the leftover grain behind anyone in whose eyes I find favor." Naomi said to her, "Go ahead, my daughter." So she went out, entered a field and began to glean behind the harvesters. As it turned out, she was working in a field belonging to Boaz, who was from the clan of Elimelek.

So Boaz said to Ruth, "My daughter, listen to me. Don't go and glean in another field and don't go away from here. Stay here with the women who work for me. Watch the field where the men are harvesting, and follow along after the women. I have told the men not to lay a hand on you. And whenever you are thirsty, go and get a drink from the water jars the men have filled." At this, she bowed down with her face to the ground. She asked him, "Why have I found such favor in your eyes that you notice me – a foreigner?" Boaz replied, "I've been told all about what you have done for your mother-in-law since the death of your husband – how you left your father and mother and your homeland and came to live with a people you did not know before. May the Lord repay you for what you have done. May you be richly rewarded by the Lord, the God of Israel, under whose wings you have come to take refuge."

– Ruth 2: 1 – 3, 8 – 12 (New International Version)

Humanity seems to have some basic disagreements. We want what we have. We want incentives to improve our own lives and those of others. We want everyone to be Ok. We want a social or financial safety net. We want people and businesses to care about customers and not exploit them or the environment. We do not want all to suffer just so some may prosper. We do not want innovation stifled by excessive rules nobody understands, let alone can follow. We want to prevent theft and other crimes. But these seem contradictory. So, we are at each other's metaphorical throats. The issue is not so much the goals of all, as these tend to be noble. It is that we seem unable to agree on one clear solution or set of solutions to resolve all the goals.

What should be the basic structure and goals of the rules, people, and organizations (government and others) who enforce the rules, from taxes to social welfare transfer payments especially? Answers can come from reasoning, religion, faith, experience, and emotion. But, experience says that less noble motives can drive, like a thirst for power, significance, influence for gain, and many other vices. When this happens it is disastrous. The Hitlers, Stalins and Maos of history, mass murderers, are clearly not the preferred choice. Even mere lower competence and professionalism can damage the lives of many people. Consider the trust and reliance we place on the Federal Reserve or other national central banks to lower or raise interest rates at just the right time and rate. We go to war, or make sweeping policy declarations negating the choice of citizens in markets.

What if the person or group making the decisions makes an error? Worse yet, what if a charlatan, actually seeking ill upon a nation gets in power, perhaps snuck in? Terrorists, and "enemies" of any country, for example, desire this. As a design engineer, I always preferred a system performing well naturally, over one needing measurement and control to do so. This avoids flaws, whether natural, or maliciously inflicted. What if wealth redistribution can happen voluntarily, without disaster from above, and without people spending their increasingly valuable time on politics, trying to make it work? Young people seek simple, technological solutions freeing of time and effort. Shall we do that especially for old problems we should have solved millennia before the Common Era, or last century at the latest?

Considering these things, I became fascinated by scriptures accepted by all three major monotheistic religions that seemed to be wise and heartfelt, covering at least the major, and possibly many of the less obvious noble goals in this set of desires by all truly concerned citizens.

Much has been claimed about what rules God might want for civil government, our interaction with civil government and its laws. They can be of the sort to advocate for obedience, or can be for at least passive non – compliance in some cases. A widely accepted type of statute is the regulatory law or edict intended to prevent some people from victimizing others (or lesser extremes of this). One danger, however, is that zeal in the theory can, with the deadly force of government, be turned into a weapon for some to thwart the efforts of, or even eliminate others for ill cause, not just good reason.

A key type of ordinance or edict is oriented to controlling morality, or the actions of others having a differing opinion about what can or should be done. It was long the case that much oppression was at least in the camouflaged cloak of such morality. It is for this reason that America, at her founding, and often since, has sought to separate church from state.

But there is another goal, perhaps more direct, relating to the welfare of people, either all people, or of a subset "belonging" to the group (Fascism, an example being the Nazi or National Socialist party in Germany), but others being any nation seeking to plunder or in lesser extreme form, benefit from resources of others.

The others can reside without the nation (and be a target for war, etc.), or within the nation (examples being slavery, Dhimmitude, where non – Muslims pay tribute to a Muslim – dominated state to be allowed to stay, but have reduced rights compared with the majority or at least ruling "type", and Nazi Germany, against not only Jews, but also many other groups considered a threat to the state of the fatherland, and also the Soviet Union). Though Communism and Fascism tend to be viewed as being on opposite ends of a spectrum, perhaps including liberal / conservative or left / right polar opposites, in practice the actual policy implementation has tended to be similarly enforced by violence. And the goal is surprisingly similar, the welfare of either "all people" or "the citizens" (Aryan race, etc.) for which the ruling is stated to be benefiting.

With globalization, this seems to tend toward policy on the socialism spectrum, though globalization has also brought to worldwide attention the version of preference for one group (Muslims over Christians and Jews, but also other "infidels" in the view of those holding these goals). Christians and Jews have likewise had practices like these in history. Indeed, in especially Old Testament scripture, it could be viewed that God seemed to like up to and including genocide for the purpose of taking, for "His chosen people", land and other property originally owned by others. And of course, the list of times when this sort of choice prevailed by many religions and empires, is quite extensive.

This can lead to a forced form of what we might call benevolence (Communism and lesser extremes on the Socialism spectrum), again, that can be quite attractive in its theoretical expounding, and is able to fuel popular uprisings of either political or sometimes violent revolutionary conflict (and of evolutionary and political progression). These very desirable, attractive matters of the overall well - being of every citizen valued in the culture and in the political inside group seem to be the major sources of merit most of the makers of laws desire when they enact such laws. So, as an engineer who likes to solve big problems others consider to be intractable, I began musing about these issues, searching for an answer all parties could like and get behind.

I became fascinated by the wisdom of God in a few scriptures (two prime examples being quotes at the beginning of this chapter). This gives an amazingly insightful solution to a prime reason that citizens commission governments to act on their behalf, yet miraculously avoids the need for much government to gather its benefits. This clearly relates to delivering economic well - being. This elegant design exemplifies "voluntary collectivism", a term I first heard from Colin

Gunn at the second Christians for Liberty conference[ii], though I have not seen a formulation of it like this one in recent history.

The goal is people working together to make sure everyone is Ok financially; can meet basic needs. But we greatly prefer this in a format that does not require government or other coercion. It encourages people to voluntarily share since it benefits them should a need arise, as inevitably happens some time in life. It is market based and leads people to encourage friends to join.

But I think, upon further reflection, this also helps the "regulation" aspect citizens also ask of government. Of these, we will explore first and primarily, the economic redistribution aspect of these answers intended to secure economic goals.

The ancient practice being discussed here is gleaning. It was enabled by the giving or sharing allowed by the owners of productive assets, during that time, of fields, vineyards, olive groves, and other agricultural assets. God wanted and ordered this as recorded in Leviticus, and other scriptures especially in the Pentateuch (first five books of what Christians now call the Bible). But it was also practiced as evidenced, for example, in Ruth chapter 2. Additionally, even religious practice in the Indian sub – continent included giving by devotees so that their spiritual teachers, at least, need not burden their spiritual work with the mundane providing for their own living. Similarly, Jesus instructed his disciples, in going out to serve, to not bring provisions, but expect their hosts to provide for such needs. For those places that do not so provide, he advised shaking off the dust of their feet as a message of rebuke.

People may not have practiced much gleaning recently. No one, it seems, has suggested it in modern times. Certainly not at scale so civilizations, nations, or the world might routinely have the resources to live, let alone prosper, and have time for mission, ministry, or especially leisure and self – improvement. Some, using their own resources do. What if many more could do so? There are fundraisers, food pantries, and other examples of some of this. But it seems society has gone the way, mainly, of delegating this provision for the poor, and of "doing good" to government. The church and volunteering seem on the decline[iii]. Though the US was traditionally more generous than people in most nations, that seems to be eroding. God's suggestion for the key issue of public policy, the difference of opinion leading to the cold and other wars, political infighting, is ignored. Is there a reason, good or otherwise?

It could be, at least in part, because the transfers, even if not "profitable" for the givers, at least can secure power to those who do the redistributing; votes, and other considerations. To the extent that an original "benevolence" intent gets converted into bribes to be granted power, the value of these transfer payments becomes coopted by those wielding such power, and creates a conflict of interest the ruling class seeks to obscure.

Another key result is that the rulers live very well. And could be viewed to be replacing those of privilege they railed upon in order to gain such power. This is evident in the high living standards of kings, and the more recent Communist and Fascist dictators, and those seeking Muslim Caliphate or other ruling status. Where there is power to be had, some humans

tend to seek it. A few of those who seek power, achieve it. And they reward themselves quite handsomely once achieved in most, if not all cases.

But the powerful are empowered by the masses. Those masses seek patronage from the powerful. And at least some of them get a portion. But what if there were a way that all could be "Ok" financially and in other ways, without that power being dispensed by political operatives seeking benefits for themselves and their cronies? I think that is the question God asked in coming up with his suggestion recorded in Leviticus 19: 9 – 10. Because the solution God architected solves it masterfully.

When people are freed even partially from the threat of making a living for themselves, it enables them to follow their heart into what brings them joy. When people voluntarily do what they most enjoy, they have a chance to become expert, even world class at whatever that is. It is people like that, freed to follow passions and dreams, who can best bring value to us all, whether paid for as a product, or not, in the form of ministry or service to humanity.

Additionally, once we have a scaled sharing system operating nearly autonomously, who knows what innovative or traditional localized sharing systems might arise, like community gardens, work building shelter for those who need it, even voluntary communes of various types, to enhance sharing to those we specifically know. These kinds of practices are already operating. Think of how much better and more joy – filled these activities could be if you and everyone have no fear that by so giving and doing good, they will still have enough to meet their daily needs; indefinitely, or at least closer to that. The widow's two mites were all she had (in Luke 21: 1 - 4 and Mark 12: 41 - 44). And Jesus praised this as a great sacrifice. But what if we all had means to share and do personally for those we know and are in need?

Let us explore a bit deeper the types of problems that arise from relying on powerful people and groups (agencies, etc.) to dispense as they choose, the higher standards of living to those they designate. And we should consider how it might be changed to a better system in actual practice, one acceptable to people with strong opinions and values on different sides of the question, who normally disagree due to differences in emphasis about what is most important.

Chapter 2
HUMAN RULING DEMANDS

The most striking feature of the political state is not governments, nor constitutions, nor laws, nor enactments, nor the judicial power, nor the police; but the universal will of the people to be governed by the common weal. Take off that restraint, and no government on earth could stand for an hour.

- Albert Pike

Samuel told all the words of the Lord to the people who were asking him for a king. He said, "This is what the king who will reign over you will claim as his rights: He will take your sons and make them serve with his chariots and horses, and they will run in front of his chariots. Some he will assign to be commanders of thousands and commanders of fifties, and others to plow his ground and reap his harvest, and still others to make weapons of war and equipment for his chariots. He will take your daughters to be perfumers and cooks and bakers. He will take the best of your fields and vineyards and olive groves and give them to his attendants. He will take a tenth of your grain and of your vintage and give it to his officials and attendants. Your male and female servants and the best of your cattle and donkeys he will take for his own use. He will take a tenth of your flocks, and you yourselves will become his slaves. When that day comes, you will cry out for relief from the king you have chosen, but the Lord will not answer you in that day." But the people refused to listen to Samuel. "No!" they said. "We want a king over us. Then we will be like all the other nations, with a king to lead us and to go out before us and fight our battles." When Samuel heard all that the people said, he repeated it before the Lord. The Lord answered, "Listen to them and give them a king."

I Samuel 8: 4 – 5, 10 – 21 (New International Version)

Throughout most of the history of civilization, especially up until recently, government has been dominated by kingdoms. Large numbers of people were ruled, almost owned, by kings or monarchs, (emperor, Czar, or other name for the absolute despot). These concentrations of massive power were usually established by force, especially war, or later by succession of kingly dynasties within families. Once established, the dynasties had legacy based power, and could not easily be deposed. They normally survived until a weak king was overthrown by another conquest from without, or uprising from within. When this happened from within, often there were justifying family ties claimed to support the change, but the reality was usually enforced through combat.

This feudal system of kings, nobles beholden to the king, knights and other warriors directed by the king, and serfs ("the king's subjects", indicating his ownership of them) serving the king much as indentured slaves, all worked together to concentrate power in the hands of the king. Kings were prone to claim moral authority, up to and including being ordained by God. Church could often be characterized as largely an instrument of the state, including for goals of perpetuating compliance among the populace.

So, despite the obvious oppression of how much control the king had over "the people", the normal situation was that everyone (with rare ambitious exceptions) honored, lauded, and magnified the king. They tended to accept their lot in life as being unchangeable, so desired their king to be strong, and plunder from neighboring "other" kingdoms. This was viewed as being for the good of the kingdom, and especially of the king, but partly on their behalf to the extent that the king was either generous, or needed to bribe support, including soldiers for military might. All this buying of power and allegiance required funds derived from taxes. During this time, taxes were viewed as being for the benefit of the king and his kingdom, but there was little or nothing the subjects could do, or expect to ever be different. Alternately, the vast majority of production might just belong to the king, with him doling it out as he saw fit. Control and ownership were very concentrated. The economy, as well as all of society was highly centralized, under the control of the monarchy.

But there were notable objections to this system, even long before the Common Era. In I Samuel chapter 8, we see Samuel relaying to Israel, God's warning of what a king would do if they chose that over the system of local Judges they had at the time. In part it was:

> "This is what the king who will reign over you will claim as his rights: He will take your sons and make them serve with his chariots and horses, and they will run in front of his chariots. Some he will assign to be commanders of thousands and commanders of fifties, and others to plow his ground and reap his harvest, and still others to make weapons of war and equipment for his chariots. He will take your daughters to be perfumers and cooks and bakers. He will take the best of your fields and vineyards and olive groves and give them to his attendants.

He will take a tenth of your grain and of your vintage and give it to his officials and attendants. Your male and female servants and the best of your cattle and donkeys he will take for his own use. He will take a tenth of your flocks, and you yourselves will become his slaves. When that day comes, you will cry out for relief from the king you have chosen, but the Lord will not answer you in that day."

– I Samuel 8: 11 – 18

But Israel refused to listen, and God let Samuel choose Saul to satisfy their clamoring for a king. Neither choosing a king, nor most individuals chosen for this honor, worked out well for Israel. Some of the kings of Israel are reported in scripture to have done "that which is right in the sight of the Lord". Things were much better during such times. But most did "that which was evil in the sight of the Lord", with dire consequences for Israel. Even David, the "Man after God's own heart", had totally faithful Uriah the Hittite, murdered by withdrawn support in the heat of the battle. Why? It was all to cover up David's illicit affair with Bathsheba, Uriah's wife. And the great Solomon, who asked God for wisdom over selfish goals, and despite David's support for his ascension to the throne, still gained power through assassinating enemies and had serious excesses in his life, if not outright flaws. Power corrupts; absolute power corrupts absolutely, even the best of humanity. In wanting a ruler, or any government, a nation places great trust in that person

or ruling group, despite this susceptibility to moral degradation due to the very power entrusted to them.

God wanted Israel to voluntarily leave grain in the edges of the fields, and grapes in vineyards for those in need. This is the perfect complement to his desire that they not choose a king to force royal policy on the people. God wants voluntary benevolence, not centrally forced collectivism.

And these two are in competition, indeed being at war with each other. One detracts from the other. Both God and the State know it. Or at least the state grows to behave as if they understand this, even if only subconsciously. This war on faith, let us call it, is especially true in most modern forms of government collectivism and cronyism including Communism and Fascism, as well as less concentrated steps along the path to these extremes in political ideology.

The similarity of the Feudal system, serfs, king, and lords, with socialist and fascist benefactors of the poor or of the favored Aryans, and with slave owning plantation operators in Dixie, are all quite striking. All are the same system, adapted to various situations.

During the Enlightenment, among its offspring, such as Freemasonry, monarchy became unpopular in some regions, notably in the American colonies and in France. These led to American and French Revolutions respectively, with differing long term success. The goal of these movements was liberty or freedom for the common people. The enlightened, educated, informed populace, wanted to determine their own destiny, and saw little value in sending the fruits of their labor across the Atlantic, then an enormous barrier. Or even within a nation to its capital in Paris.

In such a situation, the American Colonies

architected a representative governmental system and the "rule of law" to replace the central control by an individual person. They included also the limitation on democracy of a constitution, and of "checks and balances", dividing power among three branches of government, and in other ways. I have come to believe this was the best they could then come up with, but the constitution and checks and balances mainly serve to slow the degradation the founders knew historically happens in Democracies as a natural matter of course. When the majority learn they can force payments to themselves, from resources originally by the minority, they will so legislate. The same is true, perhaps just more slowly, in a representative republic, with checks and balances. And, if necessary, the majority or their representative(s) will either change the constitution, or ignore its provisions as inconvenient to their desired "reforms". All these things only delay the inevitable destruction of a nation that typically takes about a quarter to a third of a millennium, if allowed to progress naturally.

2016 – 1776 = 240 years.

Many who love America the way she was founded, including as a constitutional representative republic, think going back to those founding principles is sufficient to solve "the problems". Though I also highly value these principles and structures, I do not share that optimism of their full efficacy. These factors are political dogma, and are unable to solve the actual problems causing these issues, plus the structures are much less important than some believe. Both of these realities were touched upon by Albert Pike:

> The most striking feature of the political state is not governments, nor constitutions, nor laws, nor enactments, nor the judicial power, nor the police; but the universal will of the people to be governed by the common weal. Take off that restraint, and no government on earth could stand for an hour.
>
> – Albert Pike

Structures cannot save. But changing the will of the people to be governed by their consciences, or by benefactors can totally change the game. The reason people want the common weal Pike mentions, is they think that alone is what will make themselves or others financially Ok; secure in their futures. If so, they will sell their souls to be governed by that other giver, or even just promiser, of security.

But if there was a market based shared risk service, then citizens might prefer freedom and self – determination over slavery to "plantation owners" in far off Washington DC or another capital of their particular nation. Those who want to "do good" with the money of others, so they can charge lobbyists for access, or otherwise benefit from their power to spend "the people's" money. Or even to do the good they want to do without convincing the actual suppliers of that money to agree.

With sharing, the slaves or serfs may cooperate less, especially in this era of instant communication. With sharing, why "be governed by the common weal"? Under sharing perhaps, "no government" (or wealth redistribution program or scheme) "could stand for an hour". Why give up liberty for something (sufficient "handouts") you have already?

Chapter 3
MEANS OF PRODUCTION

Intellectual and political debate about the distribution of wealth has long been based on an abundance of prejudice, and a paucity of fact.

– Thomas Piketty, *Capital in the Twenty First Century*, P. 2.

The man who has gone through a college or university easily becomes psychically unemployable in manual occupations without necessarily acquiring employability in, say, professional work.... All those who are unemployed or unsatisfactorily employed or unsatisfactorily unemployable drift into the vocations in which standards are least definite or in which aptitudes and acquirements of a different order count. They swell the host of intellectuals ... whose numbers increase disproportionately. They enter it in a thoroughly discontented frame of mind. Discontent breeds resentment. And it often rationalizes itself into ... social criticism ... [and] moral disapproval of the capitalist order.

– Joseph A Schumpeter, from *Can Capitalism Survive? Creative Destruction and the Global Economy* pp. 173–175

For capitalism and democracy to survive, society must find a way to mitigate the social costs of a (relatively) free market economy.

– Peter Drucker

God stated his Public Policy in Leviticus 19: 9 and 10 in the Law of Moses. This was in the range of 1000 years (roughly) Before the Common Era (Before Christ). About three millennia ago. Ruth gleaned in the fields of Boaz around 2.5 Millennia back. Sharing (or gleaning) is thus an ancient precept, outlined in the context of a mostly agricultural economy. The main productive assets were then fields and vineyards. There were transportation, weapon, and warfare "industries".

But there have since then been various economic "revolutions", the Industrial Revolution being widely identified, considered singularly transformative, being more unique when it occurred. But similar revolutions occurred before the industrial revolution and since. Agriculture grew of hunter – gatherers congregating and seeking greater efficiency producing food. Empires grew, as we touched on, from conquests of neighboring peoples. There were stone, bronze, and iron ages with progressively durable and effective tools and weapons. Revolutions in knowledge and technology transformed life; manufacturing, service, transportation, medicine, communications, computing; the list goes on and on.

For simplicity and ease of dealing with this complexity, economists talk about land (including minerals and other resources of the land), labor, and capital as the raw inputs to the economy or "factors of production"[iv][v][vi], often including entrepreneurship as another explicit factor.

This is because entrepreneurs arrange the other factors to advantageously produce the goods and services we will buy, driven by the profit motive to optimize output per unit input or cost. They leverage technology, which could be viewed as yet another factor of production.

The predominant inputs to production have changed as economic revolutions have dramatically transformed the economy. 2.5 to 3 Millennia ago, Land dominated the inputs to Gross Domestic Product (a measure of the economy, not recorded then). Labor was also significant, hence the desire of kings to control land and peoples. These were the inputs to building royal power, adding to the king's standard of living.

Henry Ford, for example, during the industrial revolution, greatly enhanced the effectiveness of labor. He applied capital, but enabled many to earn quite substantial wages from even low skilled jobs. Today, increasingly the primary input is capital (technology and entrepreneurship excepted). Application of technology by entrepreneurs has reduced the labor required to produce goods, and deliver services. The graph below shows the fraction of GDP spent on Labor vs. time:

At one time, "labor saving devices" were valued by futurists and many people since they could deliver leisure. But there was a problem; leisure is much like unemployment (or underemployment). We now have a glut of leisure. Many are having difficulty finding work commensurate with their capabilities and aspirations. Capital is the factor that is "running away" with the trophy of economic prosperity. The rich are getting richer; the poor and middle class, poorer. The middle class is going away, becoming extinct.

Thomas Piketty, in his book, Capital in the Twenty First Century has identified two primary means of compensation that increasingly concentrate economic means in the hands of the few, to the, at least relative, exclusion of many.

The contributor of these two I understood even before reading Pikitty's book, was that wealthy people are investing, but most in the middle class, and nearly all of the poor, are not. The natural, understandable result or consequence of investing is that the invested capital increases exponentially over time. Good, even average, investments do this naturally. That is how compound interest, and especially investment returns, work. The rich are, in fact, getting richer. Exponentially over time.

But there is another reason Piketty cites that some are gathering massive wealth. This is the rise of the Supermanager[vii]. These include extremely valuable, and therefore, highly paid corporate leaders. Ones who, by virtue of the value they add, command enormous salaries and their equivalent in the form of deferred compensation. This group includes entrepreneurs who found massively successful firms based on seeing needs that can be met using new technology or business processes. Increasingly these scale across the globe, nearly from inception. Being insightful and ambitious at the right place at the right time, and with access to needed resources has always been extremely valuable. But technology and globalization increasingly make this combination ever more powerful in concentrating wealth. We need entrepreneurs who invent technology and business ventures enabling ongoing revolutions in commerce and society. But as the use of labor becomes increasingly scarce, replaced through technology, and this abetted by global scale, traditional "trickle down" effects become less effective, and less tenable as rhetoric for not forcing redistribution of more wealth through social programs than we do already.

Some object to such wealth, regardless of the value to many who use the low cost, valuable services. A growing few want tax rate increases, even without commensurate tax revenue growth, just to punish the ultra – "fortunate" (and ultra – insightful). But at least in the freely trading economy, nobody is required to use services, contribute to the wealth of another, or work for them. Better yet, if the entrepreneurs and supermanagers can share, and choose to do so, it will likely help everyone.

There are many examples throughout the history of industrialization in the US, for example, of let's say "aggressive" business people, some might, in times past, have referred to as former "robber barons", who later gave away much of their fortunes to build libraries, schools, hospitals, and other very valuable institutions, many of which we take for granted now in American society. There are now examples in operating system software and business investment industries, for example, whose ultra – rich leaders have decided to give away half their fortunes before they die, and are successfully urging others like them to do similarly.

All this supermanager and superentrepreneur pay is in addition to the normal growth of investment capital. Piketty gives data indicating about a third of the wealth inequality most places is due to investment growth, and about two thirds is due to the phenomena of supermanagers, and to a much lesser extent, from superstars, for example of film, sports, and music.

Recall, most Labor is going away. It is in decline. The middle class, relying on wages (that are going away), and the poor, depending on government (that is becoming increasingly insolvent, following the path of Greece), are also getting poorer, at least by comparison to those whose success is growing exponentially.

This trend is getting worse (as it did in Greece before us). Like Greece, we have massive unfunded pension and other "social contract" liabilities. Total unfunded public liabilities (obligations without money behind them) at time of writing, 2015, sum to over $94 Trillion in the United States[viii]. Notable contributors to this include Socialized Medicine, Medicare being behind nearly $28 Trillion, and Social Security, over $14 Trillion. Total unfunded US government liabilities are over five times the size of the $17.4 Trillion estimated 2014 US GDP[ix]. The "on balance sheet" national debt alone, at over $18.3 Trillion, exceeds GDP. All this is in addition to unfunded private pension obligations that will either not be met, or will require much pain and cost to bring to reasonable fiscal soundness.

The recent (as of publishing in late 2015) riots, unemployment, and insolvency in Greece are examples of what happens when the majority in a democracy demand to equality, to get what they were promised, or at least not be impoverished. For these reasons we absolutely require a solution. Additionally, even the wealthy should value the markets for their firms, and the reduced threat to life, limb, and resources, borne of most in the society being moderately content. So far, the dominant remedy people have turned to is Government. This is perhaps the obvious solution. Many have assumed it is the only possible answer, leading to great contention between those who emphasize the benefits of free market capitalism, and those who prefer the benefits that something closer to what equality of theoretical outcome can bring. Maybe neither is wrong. But the government "solution" has gotten us to the unsustainable Ponzi scheme situations we are in now. There should be a better way. Oh, yes, did God not have an opinion about this in Leviticus?

Might a sharing of 0.1% (10 basis points) both help the middle class and poor to do and learn about investing and capital, yet be less onerous than working (on average) nearly half our lives or work year just to pay the taxes? And if it enables the "rich" to have markets for the products of their firms, could this not be viewed as a bargain even for them, compared with creeping socialism or the threat of worse?

Might God's solution be the ultimate "Genius of the AND" creative compromise that enables meeting the free market desires of the capitalist – leaning, AND the collectivist sentiments also of the social activists? Both of which goals are completely valid. Might the world be more "Built to Last" following this Genius of the AND Big Hairy Audacious Goal design, both of which Collins and Porras advocate in their book by that title, *Built to Last*?

Chapter 4

AMERICAN EXPERIMENTAL ARCHITECTURE: LIFE, LIBERTY, PURSUIT OF HAPPINESS

After having thus successively taken each member of the community in its powerful grasp, and fashioned them at will, the supreme power then extends its arm over the whole community. It covers the surface of society with a net-work of small complicated rules, minute and uniform, through which the most original minds and the most energetic characters cannot penetrate, to rise above the crowd. The will of man is not shattered, but softened, bent, and guided: men are seldom forced by it to act, but they are constantly restrained from acting: such a power does not destroy, but it prevents existence; it does not tyrannize, but it compresses, enervates, extinguishes, and stupefies a people, till each nation is reduced to be nothing better than a flock of timid and industrious animals, of which the government is the shepherd.

Alexis de Toqueville in volume 2 of *Democracy in America*

...everybody feels the evil, but no one has courage or energy enough to seek the cure.

Alexis de Toqueville

33

    As discussed in chapters 1 and 2, the traditional
organization of society past the hunter – gatherer stage
of civilization has invariably been by ruler of some sort.
Call that person, usually "him", a king or monarch.
Even in smaller hunter – gatherer societies, that leader
of a smaller group was a tribal chief, with the same self
– appointed mandate to rule and govern.
    The American colonies were ruled by such a
monarch, King George III, ruler of England and Ireland
from 1760 to 1820[x]. George and his empire had the goal
and reality of never having the sun set on his empire.
The UK did with technology and trade what no
conqueror had done before. But George was ruling the
American colonies from a distance. It was "difficult",
shall we say, for poor, overcommitted George to
anticipate and devote sufficient time to optimize the
best interests of his subjects in the wild frontier, far
away from the highly refined and cultured society of
Europe.
    Europe, for its own part, was trying desperately
to digest the vast changes and questions arising in the
Renaissance[xi] followed by the Age of Enlightenment[xii],
where science, philosophy, and reason were replacing
widely held beliefs desired to be perpetuated by
religious and political institutions of the time. Highly
professional artisans like stone masons organized
themselves into guilds and lodges. They contracted
their services to rival kingdoms across Europe, and
developed a love of freedom, being above the former
ties to one king benefactor. Freemasons applied
symbols and logic of their operative craft to reevaluate
architectures of societal organization and "philosophy"
of morality, not just the "technology" of erecting huge,
impressive cathedrals, the mixing of chemicals and

medicines, or building machines to simplify and scale work. Technology enlightened reason and a heartfelt logic about how society should be.

This questioning and reevaluation orientation spread to America where the people were dealing with pioneer or "entrepreneurship" issues and conditions, vastly divergent from the views of long entrenched royalty in the "old world". Entrepreneurs and pioneers do not easily take to being told what taxes they should pay to justify the king keeping standing armies in those colonies to protect the colonists against themselves, perhaps harboring radical subversive notions that might threaten the highly enlightened plans of the wise king for their edification.

It is much like today. Most people just want to provide value to their fellow humans, and thereby take care of their families. We long ago replaced the king with a complex network of agencies, all knowing better than we what we should be protected from (and, oh, by the way), making a good living for themselves, telling the citizens what to do. It is like a cushy management job, commanding others, without needing to be hired or have any real responsibility for results. More later about how such attractive monopoly positions arise.

So, the colonies sought to influence the laws, and minimize the tax burdens for things they did not value. They asserted the claim, in the American Declaration of Independence, to inalienable rights of life, liberty, and the pursuit of happiness, and that these are endowed by the creator, not given at the whim of a monarch, or any government, for that matter.

The insight of the Americans about what they actually needed was ignored and rejected by King

George, leading to revolution. The colonies won. So they needed to govern themselves. Fortunately, some colonial leadership had ideas about that.

Among the classically educated, there was knowledge of democracy from the Greek City - States, notably Athens. But Democracy had not been so long - lasting. Besides, the various colonies wanted to control their own destiny, so there was power to disperse among the interested parties, not concentrate in the hands of one or a few. Previously, nations had been mostly formed by conquest and war. This nation had decided to cooperate together to form a new type of government, dedicated to human liberty. But would it work? Nobody was sure. It was just the best they had, and vastly better than all that had come before.

The Americans loathed concentrations of power, especially in the hands of one or a few. They built a fairly complex system of checks and balances, seeking to prevent any one group gaining too much power. And this included the people. There was, I believe, the valid concern that people, once seeing the power of the vote, could give themselves a "raise" out of tax money, destroying the system. The founders of America were clearly and acutely aware of the danger of single ruler tyranny. What was harder to anticipate was the threat of massive bureaucracy that could arise to rule in place of the king.

Hence the form of organization, legislation and other governance was in the form that came to be called a representative republic. They enacted a constitution, designed to prevent any group from exerting power of many types or in a number of categories, seeking to limit such powers. Of course, the constitution needed to include the ability to change (amend) it. And we have since found that the constitution can sometimes be ignored, apparently with impunity in some cases. But the American founders did the best they could, seeking, by rule of law, to prevent the accumulation of excessive power in the hands of either the few or the many.

Alexis de Toqueville, with the benefit of time, observation, and reflection, already by 1840 began to see issues in how effective the great American experiment was proving. That year, he published in *Democracy in America*, volume 2[xiii]:

> After having thus successively taken each member of the community in its powerful grasp, and fashioned them at will, the supreme power then extends its arm over the whole community. It covers the surface of society with a net-work of small complicated rules, minute and uniform, through which the most original minds and the most energetic characters cannot penetrate, to rise above the crowd. The will of man is not shattered, but softened, bent, and guided: men are seldom forced by it to act, but they are constantly restrained from acting: such a power does not destroy, but it prevents existence; it does not tyrannize, but it compresses, enervates, extinguishes, and stupefies a people, till each nation is reduced to be nothing better than a flock of timid and industrious animals, of which the government is the shepherd.
>
> – Alexis de Toqueville

That was his view back in 1840. Consider how the progression of the "net-work of small complicated rules, minute and uniform, through which the most original minds and the most energetic characters cannot penetrate, to rise above the crowd" has grown since then. Despite the dire nature of this vision back then, already growing like a cancer a mere two thirds of a century after the founding of America, the situation was better here than throughout the rest of the world. The American technology machine and economic engine of progress led to the greatest world power on earth. But, the continual growth of these bits of erosion of liberty, finally are taking their toll.

Increasingly, citizens like "a flock of timid and industrious animals" work harder and harder to serve "the shepherd" of government, that is, in turn, busy claiming to want the best for them. This takes forms of both taxes to enable government to give things to "the people", and regulations to protect the people from themselves and from each other. But both these forms of "help" are directed, in reality, by vested interests more than by the voters themselves. The formula for political success is to optimize for the benefit of the politician, three primary "resources":

1) Money. Campaign contributions. What wins elections is not serving the people, but gaining enough exposure and name recognition to get more votes than the other candidates. And using that to say things the voters like. The trick is to deliver value to lobbyists, while fooling voters, distracted by their ordinary lives, into thinking the politician has their (the voter's) best interest "in mind".
2) Votes. See #1 above about how to best get these.
3) Power. Besides being fun, power enables the exchange of value to lobbyists to gain their money and other support.

That is how the game is played. This is politics. It is how government works in our democratic republic. The founders did their best. But they tried to solve the issues of society and public policy using the tool of politics. Was that the best choice? Can politics and politicians consistently have heart, needed for any true caring? Is God in it? Is there a better way?

If we look again at the first two chapters of this book, God outlined that better way. He advised against a political solution (I Samuel 8, see chapter 2 of this book), and for an economic, voluntary benevolence system, perhaps with some caring involved (Leviticus 19, and Ruth chapter 2, as discussed in chapter 1). Shall we do that, as well as government, at least until we can do it alone, sharing prosperity voluntarily, not under compulsion?

Chapter 5
MODERN MONOPOLY PUBLIC POWER

The greatest crimes in the world are not committed by people breaking the rules but by people following the rules. It's people who follow orders that drop bombs and massacre villages.

- Banksy, Wall and Piece

So this is how liberty dies... with thunderous applause. [xiv]

- From Star Wars: Episode III - Revenge of the Sith

The American Republic will endure until the day Congress discovers that it can bribe the public with the public's money.

- Alexis de Toqueville

Happy families are all alike; every unhappy family is unhappy in its own way.

- Leo Tolstoy, beginning *Anna Karenina*

We are fast approaching the stage of the ultimate inversion: the stage where the government is free to do anything it pleases, while the citizens may act only by permission; which is the stage of the darkest periods of human history, the stage of rule by brute force.

- Ayn Rand

Leo Tolstoy started Anna Karenina with the statement, "Happy families are all alike; every unhappy family is unhappy in its own way.". Similarly, all good governments look exactly alike. They are all small governments. As Thomas Jefferson said, "That government is best which governs least.". If we first presume this might be true, and explore its validity as a hypothesis, we can examine what might and what might not be good governments on the basis of how little or how much they go about governing. We would expect the best governments to leave much of governing up to the citizens of the nation or region. It is a decision to put trust in the people. On the contrary, we would expect "less good" governments to exert much control over people.

This will be both for the purposes of preventing people being hurt by themselves, others, or the natural consequences of being human in the world. It takes different forms, depending on what specific dogmas or goals might have been used to justify the deadly powers normally wielded by government.

Oppressive dictatorships stifle the pursuit of happiness and quell the abundant life and in ways that outside observers often consider very different. We will explore the three major forms of greatest significance last century, and reemerging in the third millennium.

Dictatorial rulers normally get there either through succession, or from an original popular revolution. At some time, "the people" wanted what they are getting. That is true of both communist and fascist dictatorships (these two both being ultimately enforced through dictatorship in all cases), and even ordinary kings, as warned by God in I Samuel.

These are the ideological foes Americans have battled against last century. Now there is an additional variant, the Muslim Caliphate. It is not my purpose here to judge the Muslim faith. It is one of the three great Monotheistic religions that honor the Pentateuch, including Leviticus. But the political system associated with regions where this religion rules in a union of Mosque and state, has in many cases, led to abuse of some by others. This can happen with Christianity or another religion as well of course, and is the reason America insisted on prohibiting the establishment of any state religion. This joining of religious zeal and dogma with political deadly force of law is counter to the cherished American separation of church and state, and for very good reason.

Though the ideologies and goals are different, all these forms of government seem aberrations to good civil government that is supposed to do primarily the minimal jobs of deflecting foreign direct aggression and preventing the clear violation of the rights of some citizens by others.

In the case of communism, and its somewhat less extreme sibling, socialism, the prime dogma is that everyone should have the same as everyone else in society (except the rulers and their cronies need / want more). So, the revolution preceding communism is for everyone (around the world, but "we" can only control here) to be "treated" the same (have the same outcome regardless of work, contribution, etc.).

And of course, it never really works that way. Initiative is mostly gone, so living standards crash, and everyone other than a few "fortunate", privileged party members, is effectively poor. A graphic and extreme example of this is North Korea, compared with South

Korea, where the latter embraces enterprise and liberty, the former claims to want equality, but GDP per capita is near $1,800 (2013 est., Purchasing Power Parity)[xv], compared with South Korea at $34,100 (2013 est., PPP)[xvi], about 20 times greater in the same year.

Consider as visual confirmation, this night picture of the Korean Peninsula taken by satellite[xvii], where, the South Koreans can afford light:

Sharing, modernized from the voluntary, free will, and free market benevolence outlined in Leviticus and Ruth seems vastly and tangibly better than the communism by government coercion, that has been preserved in North Korea, very closely to the form desired by the originating revolutionaries.

The US, during much of last century had a cold war and nuclear arms race with the USSR, largely over this issue of forcing all people (of the world, being the goal) to be equal. This is a concern, in addition to any murder by these governments or their central directors.

The other ideology over which much blood was shed last century, came from the fascism of Germany, Italy, and the imperialism, as it was then termed, of Japan early in that century. These, of course, were the combatants on the other side from the US, UK, France, etc. during World War II. Germany, under Adolf Hitler, is still recognized as having murdered millions in what was called the holocaust. Though the Nazi Party, the Nationalsozialistische Deutsche Arbeiterpartei, NSDAP – the National Socialist German Workers' Party of Adolf Hitler, had "sozialistische" (Socialist) in its name, many these days view it, perhaps for political reasons, as a "right leaning" aberration, rather than Socialist. But the goals were very close to the Communists of that time, and indeed they were rivals for power at the time. The focus was local, nationalistic, and for the people of the German Fatherland. But it was for their welfare, and the German people, through democratic election, ushered in to lead them, one whose name became forever linked to represent man's inhumanity to man, plus women and children in gas chambers, all sold in the name of social policy to benefit the German people.

Last in this chapter, but not least, is the Muslim Caliphate. Though the religious or "faith" ideology of Communism tends to be atheism, and that of the "fascist" states varied, but seemed not too crucial to the political stances thereof, the Caliphate draws deep conviction and the seeming deadening of any caring for its victims, particularly through religious bigotry, and certainty of their superiority to all "infidels" who do not bow down to their particular view of their God, Allah. Indeed, Communism has its arrogance against those who are not "enlightened" to its utopian and redistributionist dogma. And the hatred of Jews by both German fascists and Soviet Communists was built in part on dehumanizing, viewing them as inferior.

We could discuss "someday" whether Jews, at least during "old testament" times might have done similarly (notably, for example, in I Samuel chapter 15, a passage that gave me pause for at least a decade following "troubling" events in my own life). But when a religion of any "brand" is, in reality, or by posturing, used to attack its victims, that is visceral and powerful in soliciting genocide and behavior similar in character, even if less extremely offensive. So, this danger must be taken seriously and with an abundance of caution.

Caliphates tend to formalize this dogma of the inferiority of the infidel into policies of mistreatment called Dhimmitude. This can include tolerating infidels within the borders without killing them (unless accused, with, or often without, proof), of some insult to the Prophet, or one of his followers, often the one making the accusation.

That is, they might be tolerated if they pay a tax for being of the "wrong" religion. This, of course, is antithetical to the separation of church and state in order to avoid the establishment of any official state religion. The reason for this is that doing so results (whether in Christianity, Islam, or Judaism) in unfair treatment for those who happen to believe, or choose differently.

But, the Caliphate seems to come to have as the prime goal, political power over anything to do with religion or worship of God, in whatever form. This is, in fact, its greatest threat. Additionally, these days, the Caliphate, Jihad, and Dhimmitude can be invoked even at the level of the warring tribe, not just within a national government. It can be practiced in a non – Muslim dominated nation or region, seeking the political conversion of the people there to Sharia Law, and Islam (but Dhimmitude can be an option offered). Or die in trying to maintain their preferred identity.

Having now discussed the Caliphate system at some length in a manner some, especially if feigning to be politically sensitive, might assert to be offensive, I want to absolutely clarify that I have no ill will toward anyone's religion, Muslim or otherwise. I love liberty. It is the political power wielding of a Caliphate or secular government; fascist, communist, or socialist, especially if willing to murder or oppress those who want a better way, that is offensive to human decency. Indeed, this book is about the solution God suggested, alternative to despotic political strongholds of the world system.

That (sharing) solution happens to be vastly more Sharia Law compliant (related especially to not requiring loans or insurance). Further, folks should be allowed to voluntarily choose, if they want, to live their lives in compliance with at least these two excellent goals and sentiments of that theory of action. I happen to understand and admire these goals, if allowed or recommended, not forced, and if not combined with honor killing, Jihad, and such things civilized humanity can no longer tolerate, if ever they could. Let us call it, in voluntary form, Sharia practice.

I very much hope sharing (or gleaning) can serve Muslims of good will who honor others they believe Allah created. Sharia practice does not tolerate usury, that was disdained under early Jewish precepts as well, especially to the poor, notably in Exodus 22: 25. Recall, Islam accepts the Pentateuch, including Exodus as valid scripture also. Sharing is a means to spread the risk in a

Sharia practice – honoring manner, without the usual financial approaches of the West, in allocating equity (allowed under Sharia Law) with bonds and debt (not permitted within Sharia precepts). And sharing helps, does not harm, or exploit the poor.

The world is way too leveraged in my view. The 2008 financial crisis was in large part, due to too much debt, and the passing of known – risky loans to "investors" therein. There is much danger and potential instability in some people providing others with money not owned by the recipients. The anti – usury and debt stance of Sharia could help the world, if we in the West learned new "technology" and practice for less reliance on "renting" of the money of others, even if we did not move to a full ban on the practice.

This prohibition on usury is known even by many westerners. What is less known in the west is that insurance products are considered Sharia – incompliant "gambling". I hope and expect to work with Muslims of good will, on sharing as a shared risk solution, not in violation of their convictions of the haram nature or undesirability of the practice of maisir[xviii], or gambling, in this case, through insurance.

There is, in sharing, no agreement for payment dependent on anything like insurance loss or peril. It is but a group of folks, agreeing to help others, including themselves recover, as a lack of resources in accounts (for whatever reason) indicates would be helpful. It is like alms and help to the poor and for all; Sadaqah[xix], as Allah loves.

I previously in this chapter, applied reasoning from apologetics, appealing to Muslims as to why my objection to the Caliphate political system does not mean I reject excellent principles of Sharia practice (if followed voluntarily). Apologetics is an explanation for having a stance[xx]. It is not saying I am sorry for having that view. I now appeal to Christians with apologetic reasoning, about why we can, and should, dialog and work with Muslims as well as others with insights we missed, perhaps including from Sharia practice.

Jesus reached out radically and shockingly in his day, to those not accepted in his culture. These include a (Good) Samaritan, of a class hated by people of his day, yet the hero of my favorite story Jesus told. Jesus talked with, and helped a Samaritan woman, with the gender gap being a social protocol violation on top of the Samaritan thing. He ate with tax collectors (who were despised in part for cheating people), and sinners, asking regarding the woman caught in adultery who, without sin, might cast the first stone, and forgiving the many sins of a woman who washed his feet with tears and precious ointment, but not those "few" of Simon, the host at dinner since he "cared little", she, much. The dream ordering Peter to eat things not kosher let us say, led to the acceptance of gentiles. We could go on and on. The great commission, last time I checked, did not bar talking to any person, in sharing good news (the meaning of "the gospel"; Mark 16: 15 uses this term). How shall they hear without someone to tell them, or teach as did Philip the Ethiopian eunuch? I bet it is not forbidden to learn from others, up to including hearing or studying some of their good news, or sharing (both directions) insights with those having very different experiences than we.

Blessed are the poor in spirit, for
theirs is the kingdom of heaven.

Blessed are those who mourn for they will be comforted.

Blessed are the meek, for they will inherit the earth.

Blessed are those who hunger and thirst for righteousness, for they will be filled.

Blessed are the merciful, for they will be shown mercy.

Blessed are the pure in heart, for they will see God.

Blessed are the peacemakers, for they will be called children of God.

Blessed are those who are persecuted because of righteousness, for theirs is the kingdom of heaven.

Blessed are you when people insult you, persecute you and falsely say all kinds of evil against you because of me. 12 Rejoice and be glad, because great is your reward in heaven, for in the same way they persecuted the prophets who were before you.

– Matthew 5: 3 – 12 (NIV)

Be not overcome of evil.
But overcome evil with good.

– Romans 12: 21 (KJV)

I could write things similar to these about Sharia Law forced by Caliphate on others, also to proponents of redistribution, for equalizing outcomes, or favoring, for a socially attractive reason, "our" kind of people (good Germans, good Americans, good Muslims many places, good Israelis, good Chinese, good ...) who all deserve fulfilling lives, and especially merit being able to help enhance the lives of others. May we all be gentle with each other, our beliefs and aspirations for families and daily bread, plus much more. For none of us, with possible very rare exception(s), is perfect.

In summary, various styles of government – sponsored terror exist, capable of leading to mass murder, but they are in actually not so vastly different, being mainly different "brands" and manifestations of selfishness on the part of people using these political power plays to get their way, including power and economic means. And to control the choices of others. Democrats and socially conservative Republicans fit this model also, to control the "giving" of others upon threat of harm and taking it anyway, or on controlling moral choices, respectively.

Would it not be better for these to be voluntary at least within reason? Does God not grant us free will to obey moral laws or not as we choose, though with consequences? Does not God love a cheerful giver (II Corinthians 9: 7), over one under compulsory extortion by government? Is not the voluntary charitable gift, not only more appreciated, but also vastly more effective? Is the centrally managed needs testing worth the political conflicts of interest inherent in voting for free stuff, and the profit motives to influence the powerful, by crony capitalist suppliers of free cell phones and service (at attractive gross and net margins, covered by taxpayers), subsidizing food production they could not otherwise sell, sweet financing deals for technology development or other purposes, the regulation into oblivion of attractive competitors, tax loopholes for rich and famous donors, all while claiming to be "populist", or not, etc.?

Jesus rejected the luring, siren temptation of political power to accomplish his "ends" or goals in Matthew 4: 8 – 10. May folks of all religions, origins, creeds, and social goals everywhere, do likewise.

Chapter 6
Monopoly Partnership: Crony Capitalism

Our politicians are little more than money launderers in the trafficking of power and policy – fewer than six degrees of separation from the spirit and tactics of Tony Soprano.

> – Bill Moyers

Politics is like making sausage, you don't want to know how it is done.

> – Otto van Bismark

Big government and big business are allies, not enemies, in the concentration of power.

> – Milton Friedman

No one will really understand politics until they understand that politicians are not trying to solve our problems. They are trying to solve their own problems -- of which getting elected and re-elected are No. 1 and No. 2. Whatever is No. 3 is far behind.

> – Thomas Sowell, Economist

The consumer is the only man in our economy without a high-powered lobbyist in Washington.

> – John F. Kennedy

The theory of government, as we explored last chapter, can take the form of socialism or its extreme, communism, nationalist goals in fascism, or power by those claiming religious justification, whether Muslim Caliphate, Christian monarch, or any other, for their "need" to oppress others to bring about the form of utopian society or morality being held up as the ideal at the time.

The actual running of an entire economy by the state (Communism) has been largely discredited by the fall of the Soviet Union, and the Chinese are likewise clearly practicing capitalism in some form. But how does this work when big government claims to protect "the people" from big business and other dangers? Are there drawbacks to big government forcing goodness on its people, short of mass murder? How does it work, and who benefits?

Politicians and even their predecessors, the revolutionaries, are not mainly trying to solve our problems. They are trying to solve their problems as Thomas Sowell pointed out. Politicians have very big problems. So big that they are way too busy to figure out what one person needs. The problems are hard enough, the politicians busy enough and their focus generalized enough, that they need help in figuring out what they should advocate for. Citizens are likewise too busy living their lives, and making a living, to help politicians know what is best to force upon the whole country for its own good.

But there have arisen, from the early days of the Republic, people who will spend time informing those wielding government power what they should force people to do. Not only will they inform the politicians, but they also volunteer to help finance them to get the exposure they need for their politics business to thrive and be successful. These benefactors of the politicians are called lobbyists.

If the politicians are solving their own problems, the lobbyists are even more about solving the problems assigned them by business and other interests that pay them to find political solutions for their problems. What are the problems of such business interests? It may be that perpetuating, or maximizing profits might top that list. So, it would be amusing, if it were not so tragic, that many advocate larger government to punish "evil", money grubbing rich people.

In chapter 4 we asserted that the primary jewels of the political system are:

4) Money. Campaign contributions. What wins elections is not serving the people, but gaining enough exposure and name recognition to get more votes than the other candidates. And using that to say things the voters like. The trick is to deliver value to lobbyists, while fooling voters, distracted by their ordinary lives, into thinking the politician has their (the voter's) best interest "in mind".

5) Votes. See #1 above about how to best get these.

6) Power. Besides being fun, power enables the exchange of value to lobbyists to gain their money and other support.

The system, over time, tends to go way beyond "mere" quid pro quo exchanges of campaign finance money for political, legislative, and other power. It can include jobs after office or direct payments and favors now. Especially plumb assignments after holding office can be for the lobbying of friends already made in government, once the term of office expires. This is a win – win situation for both the former politician and for the firm hiring ("compensating") them for "access" before and after leaving office. But often in conflict of interest, not such a win for citizens.

There may be rules against improper conflicts of interest with the public. But who enforces them? Is it not the politicians themselves? Enthusiastic regulators of others can tend to be vastly less diligent in regulation of their own activities. This is an inherent issue in much of government. It is difficult to get people, especially if powerful, to control their own activities. We may need a market and voluntary purchasing of services to do the regulation or selection well.

The benefactors of the benefactors of politicians tend to be large enterprises. President John F. Kennedy observed that "The consumer is the only man in our economy without a high-powered lobbyist in Washington". So, it is clearly not mainly for consumers (or call them "citizens") that special tax loopholes and regulatory provisions are carefully crafted into legislation. Similarly, small business has its hands full competing with large established firms, and just delivering a great product people will buy. There may be a few groups that claim to represent small business. But even these are likely to look for bigger, better organized sources of money to "do their job" (get paid), than is available from ensembles of small businesses, let alone individual small businesses. That, of course, does not prevent the politic claim that they are looking out for the little guy, when justifying seeking donations or other support for the cause. This makes the delivery of influence to the larger interests all the more stealthy, and therefore, effective.

So, if we realize it is big business, not small, or consumers, that gets the lion's share of the benefits of "good" big government, what do they get? Similarly, "What is the purpose of regulation?" Is it to protect consumers mainly? If we believe John Kennedy, it is not, in reality primarily to help or protect consumers. Similarly, if we follow the money, realizing it is mainly large businesses that can afford time and money to "influence" (or "guide") government, it might logically follow that most of the benefits of government action, especially regulation serve the needs of existing big business to perpetuate large returns they obviously achieved to get to that status of being a big business, some of which is expense money, a cost of business, to buy politicians. Politics and Regulation are often mainly to protect large industry from entrepreneurial firms that dare to improve on their existing way of doing things, as judged by the market.

We will discuss further how sharing can help meet the legitimate goals we have for regulation of protecting people from businesses and other problems in volume 3, about Impact.

Chapter 7

SHARING LIBERATING SOLUTIONS

Jesus crossed to the far shore of the Sea of Galilee (that is, the Sea of Tiberias), and a great crowd of people followed him because they saw the signs he had performed by healing the sick. Then Jesus went up on a mountainside and sat down with his disciples. The Jewish Passover Festival was near.

When Jesus looked up and saw a great crowd coming toward him, he said to Philip, "Where shall we buy bread for these people to eat?" He asked this only to test him, for he already had in mind what he was going to do.

Philip answered him, "It would take more than half a year's wages to buy enough bread for each one to have a bite!"

Another of his disciples, Andrew, Simon Peter's brother, spoke up, "Here is a boy with five small barley loaves and two small fish, but how far will they go among so many?"

Jesus said, "Have the people sit down." There was plenty of grass in that place, and they sat down (about five thousand men were there). Jesus then took the loaves, gave thanks, and distributed to those who were seated as much as they wanted. He did the same with the fish.

When they had all had enough to eat, he said to his disciples, "Gather the pieces that are left over. Let nothing be wasted." So they gathered them and filled twelve baskets with the pieces of the five barley loaves left over by those who had eaten.

John 6: 1 – 13

Why does sharing work? I have no earthy idea! It is not a logic thing. It is a Love thing. When the boy gave all he had, the five loaves and two fish, God multiplied it through his Son. Why were the widow's two mites worth more than all the rich people giving (Luke 21: 1 - 4 and Mark 12: 41 - 44)? Because it was what she had. And she gave it to share with others. Many rich people hoarded everything except what they thought would impress others, or satisfy the rules. They paid their voluntary "taxes", or even their tithe, to the temple. But the little boy's lunch, and the widow's two mites were greater than all those put together.

The investment returns of Jesus of Nazareth were likely better than ours. But it seems like nobody for two and a half millennia has been giving the edges of their fields, or leaving grapes in the vineyard for the poor and alien. Sharing fields, vineyards, fish, loaves, and mites is not widespread these days. So, if nobody is doing it much at all, should we not start with whatever processing gains we have at our disposal? The real question is, "Will you be part of the solution?".

One boy among 5000 men (plus women and children, maybe 20,000 or so), with the risk adjusted investment returns of Jesus fed the whole crowd, with 12 baskets left over. What if 1% of the people (say 200) shared? Maybe more did bring their own lunch next time, hoping it would be shared. What if 10% shared their lunch?

Five loaves and two fishes feeding 5000 people with 12 baskets left over is a miracle. If 2 fish and 5 loaves feed a person, compounding that at 10% per year (near long term historical stock market returns) would feed another in addition to the giver in 8 years. If you share 5 loaves and two fish each year, it will take

66 years to feed 5000 people once, given these 10% compound annual returns. Those who start early may be able to do so.

In rural communities, like where I live, we do fundraising events to help out people with health or other needs. These include catfish fries, barbeque, fried chicken (with all the fixins), silent auctions, louder auctions, and these often combined with entertainment. Big cities (and big celebrities) have been known to put on benefit concerts.

So, we already share. And we should continue to share that way. But these events take a lot of work, and enable some modest amount of benefit to flow to specific designated people. Ones we have decided merit and need our assistance. Or they serve specific causes, in the case of larger benefit concerts. They serve the needs of some people. But none of them serve even some needs of every person who could use help. All those in need must either find the source of help, or be known to the organizers of the benefit event to serve that need. It "feeds" a few people. It does not feed all men, women, and children making up the crowd of need. Is it possible we can do better?

What if we added a scalable sharing system? What if we apply the modern technology of electronic transfers and recordkeeping to a growing network of individuals who want to see abundant life and joy lived out by others in their community and world? Might others be enthused to join such a movement?

The widow's two mites, and the boy's loaves and fishes certainly did not hurt anything. They helped, according to the two stories. So, it is not a problem to do the sharing. And the more sharing that gets done, the better for more people. But, what might we expect as the "limit" of this form of sharing? As we eventually roll the snowball faster and larger downhill, what could we expect the whole global practice to bring about?

In the USA, the per capita income (2012) is near $43,000[xxi] and the wealth per adult is about $300,000[xxii]. The Global household wealth in mid-2012 totaled $223 trillion, equivalent to $49,000 per adult in the world[xxiii]. It is distributed thusly[xxiv]:

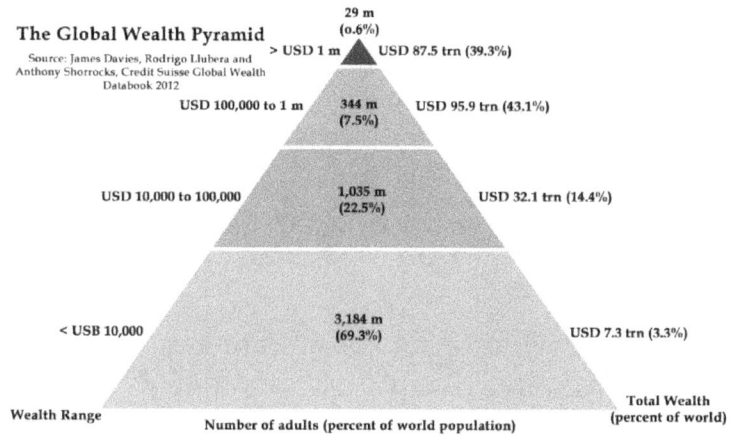

Let's use $50,000 as being near the global mean wealth per adult; what the wealth would be around the world from which people share, if they do share. This should be conservative compared with using a US average.

Sharing 0.1% (10 basis points) from an average $50,000 gives an annual sharing cash flow to a small account of $50. In 49 years that would build such an account to the present average wealth of the world. This is without any "work" or adding by the owner of that account. In a half century we can double the number of people participating in the sharing just through the sharing itself. Or that is how long it takes a new account to grow to the value of the average, if average account values stay the same rather than grow larger yet. That is, if superior investment returns more than make up the 10 basis points of sharing flows). To check this, or test your own assumptions, this is how it works:

This is a future value problem. We can enter this information into a financial calculator:

Interest	=	10%
Present Value	=	0
Payment	=	– $50 (– since assumed paid by the account)
Future Value	=	$50,000 (the amount we want to build to)

Then we solve for N, the number of years to reach that desired $50,000. It is actually the same number of years if we assume any amount for the desired final value, and one thousandth (0.1% or 10 basis points) of that amount cash flow into the recipient account annually.

Of course, the total wealth (or average wealth) of the world will be growing dramatically, as it is now. It is just that the sharing will be drawing all participants along to some reasonable fraction of that average over a half century. This is in addition to anything they do to actively to grow their own account. And at 10 basis points (0.1%), it does not hurt anyone to any observable extent.

You may not like this. A mere $50,000 shared including investment returns to those participating, and that requiring a half century. But what does it hurt to do this? Is it causing any harm? Then, how does this compare with all the social programs ever funded by taxpayer money, or even those given through churches, charities, or other groups? Might enhanced results happen even without Jesus being present? How?

Should we, like children with a lunch of loaves and fishes, share in the hope that this minor miracle just might become massively more major? If the investment returns are about the 10% long term gain of the stock market (with nothing added above what is taken out, and of course, more will likely be added than removed), then the wealth of the world will double (or more) in 8 years. So, as the sharing is bringing up all the smaller than average accounts, the (average) amount in existing accounts it is approaching will be increasing dramatically.

Well, now consider that the $50,000 (and the additional doubling on average in eight years) is added to whatever a person might grow in their account anyway. If they are adding $50 per month ($600 per year), then THAT PERSON grows their account from zero to $50,000 in 24 years. About half the time from sharing alone.

Suppose that person takes $26 of that growing capital available, and sells collared greens in Kibera, a large slum in Nairobi Kenya, as Tabitha Atieno Festa did to build a start for her dream of founding a medical clinic there[xxv]. And it led to the founding of Carolina for Kibera, a growing nonprofit organization helping people live better lives in Kibira. Tabbitha has gone on from this earth. But her legacy and inspiration continue in the lives of those in her city, and around the world.

This illustrates that the half century returns from

the stock market required to bring all to the present average wealth per capita of the world, may vastly underestimate the growth of many entrepreneurial ventures that some individuals might build with the sharing. And employment or alliances those enterprises may build for and with others. This increase in the need for labor, due to entrepreneurship and innovation can build jobs and grow the sharing asset base much more rapidly than the simple public market investment case calculated above.

How many are fed, have medicine, or get an education because of that $26 given to Tabitha? If we have a means of scaling up benevolence of this type, will we not do it? If we estimate the progress to be slower than we want, will we not start as soon as we possibly can? We may find other miracles happen also. People set free to give, to work, and to contribute as they want, without fear of losing a needs testing status and "free stuff" handouts may contribute way beyond what we expect they might.

Shall we not do it?

Chapter 8

LIFE, LIBERTY, JOY

We hold these truths to be self-evident, that all men are created equal, that they are endowed by their Creator with certain unalienable Rights, that among these are Life, Liberty and the pursuit of Happiness. — That to secure these rights, Governments are instituted among Men, deriving their just powers from the consent of the governed, — That whenever any Form of Government becomes destructive of these ends, it is the Right of the People to alter or to abolish it, and to institute new Government, laying its foundation on such principles and organizing its powers in such form, as to them shall seem most likely to effect their Safety and Happiness.

- Declaration of Independence, United States of America

Any institution which does not suppose the people good, and the magistrate corruptible, is a vicious one.

- Maximilian Robespierre[xxvi]

The thief cometh not, but for to steal, and to kill, and to destroy: I am come that they might have life, and that they might have it more abundantly.

- Jesus the Christ, as recorded in John 10: 10, KJV

1) Do no harm.
2) Do good.
3) Stay in Love with God.

- John Wesley, stating his three simple rules[xxvii]

High expectations are the key to everything.

- Sam Walton

It seems much has gone wrong these days in the land of the free and the home of the brave. The founders wanted to place a great deal of trust in liberty to enable a worthy and fruitful, fulfilling life, and the pursuit of happiness. Ideally, that could still be the case. But is liberty some utopian dogma of a Shangri La that is impossible to actually do, and still avoid the ills of people starving in the streets, total destruction of the environment, and white collar criminals cheating your neighbor and you out of hard earned savings, Madoff in pyramid investment Ponzi scams?

The crux of the matter is, "Who do you trust?". Maximilian Robespierre, in stating "Any institution which does not suppose the people good, and the magistrate corruptible, is a vicious one.", says that the people might be more reliable than the magistrate in ensuring goodness to neighbor. It is in concert with the admonition that power corrupts. And absolute power corrupts absolutely.

John Wesley, founder of Methodism had three simple rules.

1) Do no harm.
2) Do good.
3) Stay in love with God.

Does government do no harm? It can be easy to not bother to look for, and therefore not recognize harm in seeking to perform a mission. But scarier yet is the question, "Does government mind doing harm, even purposely, if this is "collateral damage" in its crusade to 'do good'?".

This "Who do you trust?" issue is crucial. There are at least two questions about it related to politics.

1) Will that individual or group actually do what they say, or will they instead serve their own interests, be incompetent, be treasonous to the cause they claim (which can happen), or otherwise be an all powerful (or too powerful) problem rather than the all powerful solution we all (or about half of us) are looking for?

2) How long will this "benevolent dictatorship" continue to be benevolent in the hands of the subsequent rulers or central planners once these are gone?

There is a massive body of history of promises by government that this political dogma or that political operative will conduct the best top down management and make "you" equal with others, or safe from "those people", or will bring about the glorious empowering of the home nation. But empires are not thousand year Reichs typically. Most last at most about a third of a millennium. Many wax belligerent, and are destroyed by the neighboring nations they terrify, or implode from within. All this despite the fact that many such tyrants were democratically elected. Then they just decided getting their agenda done was more important than laws or other inconvenient obstacles.

It is crucial for long term success, that a solution people want, be inherently resistant to abuse. We want something that tends to naturally "Do no harm.", as Wesley considered imperative. One way to prevent a great deal of the type of harm we are discussing is to diffuse, not concentrate power, especially deadly force no citizen or group can resist.

Said another way, it is massively desirable if we can come up with a market based process that actually does good. This will then naturally diffuse the power among many participants competing with each other to do that good, instead of an all – powerful monopoly we hope will do our collective bidding and do good without harming many. We want this condition to persist through generations.

Even voluntary charity can bring harm to the poor.[xxviii] This is due to the consequences of even that voluntary charitable system segregating people, we might say, Jim Crow style, into haves and have nots, to the perpetual harm to those trapped as designated have – nots due to needs testing. Consider what greater harm might derive from forcing something that, even with voluntary limits on scope, can perpetuate.

Oh, the "have nots" in some cases, may use welfare and similar payments from taxpayers as capital to finance criminal activities from human trafficking and murder on down, since proceeds of these are not taxed, nor do they prevent continued taxpayer support, being undetected by needs testing.

More importantly, with sharing, perhaps some will no longer need crime to survive. Sharing just might enable that alternative stance that we may again be able to trust people to overwhelmingly do the right thing, being empowered to safely do so.

Sharing might let people be good most of the time (especially, more of the time) than they would be under millions of words of tax code and threat of financial ruin (or some places, in some regimes, death) for noncompliance. Regardless of their need, because we "must" make sure the poor get their fair share?

Elephants in Africa are in danger of going extinct. That is because a poor person there with no other means of support can shoot one, extract its tusks, leave the rest to rot, and sell the tusks to the Chinese to make the intricate lovely carvings they are known for. Even the Chinese are becoming concerned about this. Would that wantonness occur, if the poacher had means of support? I say some former poachers, if Ok financially, might instead work hard to preserve the elephant population. This is just one example.

Suppose we, as a community of investors, freely and voluntarily teach everyone to cultivate their own field of capital, and live off proceeds from investment returns of that capital. If they know they must be careful with it, and there is no needs testing, they can work (as poor people always have) to subsist, while building a better life, helped automatically by others. This can be enhanced by charitable groups already in existence, or others empowered by new folks with capital built by compound investment returns and sharing transfers. These groups will learn (and need to learn) that it is crucial they help people become self – supporting, not just give handouts. Charity can be damaging to self – worth, and the ability of many in this "needs tested" category to ever escape squalor[xxix].

Sharing jettisons needs testing. It can be viewed as an equity based form of microfinance, superior to the microloan "first generation" microfinance for which Muhammad Yunis[xxx], founder of Grameen Bank[xxxi], in Bangladesh won the Nobel Peace Prize. With sharing of micro equity, there is no need for a loan adjustment overhead monitoring function. We simply trust people to not blow the small cash flow building their field of capital on something stupid. It is Ok if they do that. It will not hurt the system. It is not to their benefit, but recall we are building a system that empowers people, even the poor, to take responsibility for themselves. We expect people (as my parents did me) to be responsible. And psychological testing has indicated that people rise to meet high expectations[xxxii]. Sam Walton said "High expectations are the key to everything.".

So, what will happen with sharing is that some in communities around the world will grow capital in the public markets, and also develop microenterprises. Others will observe these new firms and entrepreneurs, perhaps partner with them, and grow their own dreams of success. Meanwhile, the entire network will be getting stronger from each success anywhere in the world. There has long been a fear among some of government at a world – wide scale, directed from above where all are subservient to the global ruler. But this is not like that. There is no coercion in this free market part of the system. Nobody need get any mark on their person to trade. It is only supportive, not coercive in any manner. The "Do no harm" aspect of sharing is intact. So, any who want regulation, taxation, and even fining for not buying crony capitalist, state sponsored products, can argue their case. It is just that most such nonsense will be rejected by folks newly empowered with viable economic opportunity and especially the dream of a chicken in every pot (or whatever they like to eat).

Oh, there is one other thing. If the investment returns on average are somewhat higher, the 10 basis points of sharing (0.1%) can be further unnoticeable. Often when I talked to people about sharing early in the development process, their eyes glazed over. They seemed to want to know what would happen with their money, even if left unstated. So, I designed a stock selection and portfolio management system based on quantitative fundamental analysis to seek undervalued securities and lead to superior risk adjusted investment returns. Back tested to before the financial meltdown of 2008, the process would have behaved as shown below against a benchmark of the Russell 3000 Index.

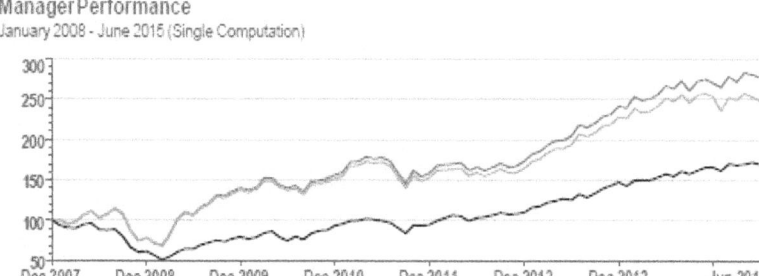

Manager Performance
January 2008 - June 2015 (Single Computation)

— StockRoller Domestic Gain (Gross) StockRoller Domestic Gain (Net) — Russell 3000

Past results do not indicate or guarantee future performance. The investments can lose money. They did during some time periods.

Incidentally, research indicates[xxxiii] that within a client and financial advisor collaboration, the effective information processing, a realistic self-assessment, a tolerance for pain, and empathetic communication all contribute to portfolio outperformance, as well as the superior meeting of financial goals in life by a given level of resources. So, it helps substantially, to look circumspectly at investments over a long time period, applying emotional intelligence, tolerating pain when it inevitably comes at some point.

But, if long term returns tend to do better than other investments a person could make, that can help, including covering any "cost" to a wealthy investor of sharing with others. Some might view the 0.1% or 10 basis points of sharing almost like a free service.

There is not enough capital in the world to support every person on the planet with a mere 0.1% of it per year. So, a government tax on capital will not do the job. You next would–be Stalin, Hitler, or Mao, just forget about it. You will not get it to work. You will just Madoff with the money and power. And we no longer want that. Or your stinking needs testing for the purpose of controlling us.

Seriously, shall we start sharing now and see how good it could be with this change of assumptions about who can be trusted, those who share, or those who redistribute? What have we to lose? Other than corrupt magistrates, no longer able to limit our dreams, love, and joy, sapping our power to personally improve the world through work and investments we select? Shall we consider a voluntary, free market sharing to help ourselves and others, in addition to doing so through taxes and the restriction of our choices in life? Or perhaps eventually, do so instead of that way. Would this bring more liberty, as well as better results? Might we then have more time for family, to do work, play, and good, leading to greater joy in life?

Chapter 9
INTEGRATING FINANCIAL SERVICES

Everything should be made as simple as possible, but not simpler.

- Albert Einstein

Necessity, they say, is the mother of invention. We have a lot of necessity in our society today. And I think the time is here for inventing new approaches, new solutions for these various problems, so that we can indeed maintain America, and indeed the rest of the world as well, as the land of opportunity for all of those who will be the achievers of the future.

- Robert Noyce[xxxiv]

The Government is an insurance company with a standing army.

- Ezra Klein

I try to buy stock in businesses that are so wonderful that an idiot can run them. Because sooner or later, one will.

- Warren Buffett

He that is of the opinion money will do everything may well be suspected of doing everything for money.

- Benjamin Franklin

Do not save what is left after spending, but spend what is left after saving.

- Warren Buffett

The purpose of financial services is to serve people, to meet their various financial needs and goals. In general, people prefer simplicity, transparency, and effectiveness. They want the products to work. They want their money to grow. They want, in many cases, various risks mitigated, shared with others, perhaps through insurance of various types. Some may like the idea of giving to family members, charities, and even others they may or may not know well, but have need of the financial help. There may be tax implications, where clients prefer to minimize their taxes to spend, invest, or give their resources as they want, rather than as a central planner sees fit. This is complex and all encompassing. Can we address it all simply and easily?

Intel and semiconductor firms integrated many data processing and communication functions onto integrated circuit chips last century. This millennium, we seek integration of the financial services sector of the economy, applying the wisdom of Intel cofounder Bob Noyce in observing:

> Necessity, they say, is the mother of invention. We have a lot of necessity in our society today. And I think the time is here for inventing new approaches, new solutions for these various problems, so that we can indeed maintain America, and indeed the rest of the world as well, as the land of opportunity for all of those who will be the achievers of the future.
>
> – Robert M Noyce

At present, much about financial services and designating what is to happen with money or capital is complex. There is much paperwork up to and including court action needed especially when a loved one passes. Much of this is left over from decades, if not centuries past. It helps lawyers, accountants, financial planners, and insurance people, (even tax collectors and adjusters because people have not used all the legal provisions of the tax code to minimize paying tax). In choosing this, it is helpful if it all integrates together as sharing does inherently. This integration enables less paperwork and distractions at a time of grieving loss, as well as throughout life in general.

Let's talk about insurance. The purpose of insurance is as a shared risk mitigation tool. A pool of insurance customers shares the risk of perils, hazards, and actual losses collectively among policy holders. But insurance products are what I call point solution products. Meaning insurance companies very carefully carve out precisely what they are, and are not liable to cover. And they, with very careful attention to detail, write this into the detailed insurance contracts. A prime example is flood insurance. It has been repeatedly broadcast on Television that, if a flood occurs, and you have not paid for flood insurance, the insurance firm owes you precisely nothing. This is Ok (certainly legal), you are supposed to read the ten page contract and know this. But my point is that insurance is generally written to benefit the insurance company, not the client (who they call "policyholder", a party to whom the insurance firm can become adversarial once there are claims payments at stake).

This brings up another couple costs of insurance. The insurance firm builds a policy underwriting bureaucracy for the purpose of screening out potential policyholders who might be more likely than average to actually make claims, and a claims adjustment bureaucracy to reject actual claims on the insurance product. Insurance is best paid for, not used, from the insurer's perspective. So they charge good policy premium money to policy holders to make as certain as they can that this is usually the case. It is a conflict of interest between the insurance company and you, as customer.

The differing opinions can become even stronger, requiring the customer to find a lawyer and sue the insurance company to get what the customer thinks is owned on a policy claim. It is common for the insurance firm and adjusters to hope the policy holder either just gets tired of hassling with them, does not know their rights, or otherwise "blinks". But a good lawyer who advertises on TV may be able to extract payment from insurance companies. The thing is they charge about a third of the "take" IF, and only IF they consider it worth their bother, and it may take months to actually get the money. The client pays the insurance firm's lawyer, their lawyer, and previously mentioned overhead bureaus of the insurance firm to protect themselves from the claims of policyholders, before they ever get anything that is the actual value to the claim receiver of having insurance at all.

Another way to describe this is that insurance is another form of needs tested transfer payment. There are government, as well as private firm, needs testing (claims adjustment) variations. Ezra Klein went so far as to say the US Government is an insurance company with a standing army, clearly indicating the extent to which "Uncle Sam" has a "take care of you" service, for which "he" charges good money, somewhere in the range approaching half of everything the average worker makes in salary. Plus Sam, and his brand, is a monopoly, having no competition. Sam furthermore makes the rules under which he operates, including the ability to exclude other competitors by law. Show me a monopoly that would not like that. The government also runs some perhaps beneficial insurance pools with disaster risk coverage no company could bear, only a sovereign nation.

Insurance is a complex system. This does not mean insurance firms are necessarily made up of bad people. Though there can be some that seem to qualify as dishonest, but likely most follow the law usually. The conflict of interest with this approach seems inevitable. And indeed, it has replaced much of fraternal benevolence as another means we once had as a substantial alternative, and government may have had an incentive and hand in its demise. But, at least for many years, insurance has seemed to be the best thing we had to mitigate risk through sharing that risk. Most may be just doing their job the best way they can. Insurance may just be old technology.

Let's compare and contrast this with sharing. Sharing does not prevent any other systems, insurance, government, or otherwise. It does no harm. You can still buy policies, and we all must, at present, spend part of our time in slave labor to government to do free accounting services for them in reporting taxes, so we can pay them. Though the Fair (consumption or sales) Tax emancipates from that, and is vastly superior from a global competitive perspective (taxing foreign goods and services at the cash register, and NOT taxing domestically produced products for export). Sharing works in the background. Unlike many needs tested systems, including insurance, no paperwork or decision stands in the way of delivering service. It is simple, has little or no paperwork, approval, court or other delays, so clients can focus on life. Simplification is always good, especially in times of stress or sorrow. It makes management easier, and the service more compelling.

But simple services are also easier for the supplier to deliver. They tend to be more foolproof and robust; higher quality. This is especially true if the firm need not make many decisions in its delivery of service. Warren Buffett said "I try to buy stock in businesses that are so wonderful that an idiot can run them. Because sooner or later, one will.". This presumably applies to his insurance firms as well. But insurance companies are complex. They must be managed well to prosper, and continue providing service. Sharing, by contrast, serves naturally, in the face of a vast portfolio or array of risks. All in a way "even an idiot can run", not requiring minute micromanaging by StockRoller or expense delivering the risk management service by the simple sharing among clients.

And of course, there is huge value to clients if they can minimize time, mental effort, consternation on exactly what to buy and how much, etc., becoming expert in the arcane arts of insurance hazards, perils, fullness of coverage, various forms of deductibles, etc. The simplicity of sharing, but power of its ability to cover a portfolio of many types and aspects of risk management, unlike any particular insurance type, may be more easily managed by both client and supplier, and is scalable to provide better, more comprehensive service. And may do so for the benefit of all stakeholders, even clients.

Sharing is not specific about what kind of risk or

peril it can address. It can help with opportunities and nearly all needs, including ones that cannot be insured at all. Sharing continues as long as there are participants in the sharing network. Sharing, however, does not cover any big loss immediately. You can still get insurance for that, and it is often a good idea. But the sharing does not "pay off big" at a given time. It is instead a slow cash flow that helps build back a client account, whose owner has been under financial stress. But the sharing cash flows are intended to be based on entire lifetime investment accounts of many, later most investors in the network. So, the investment accumulations can be substantial.

All insurance payments typically come out of lifetime earnings. They are small compared with what a person should accumulate over a lifetime of investing. But the sharing is intended to build up over time, a base of capital about the same size as an average wealth accumulation. This, then, is much more than the total insurance payments over a lifetime. It may be able to solve more problems better than insurance ever could.

I will further explain this graph in volume 2:

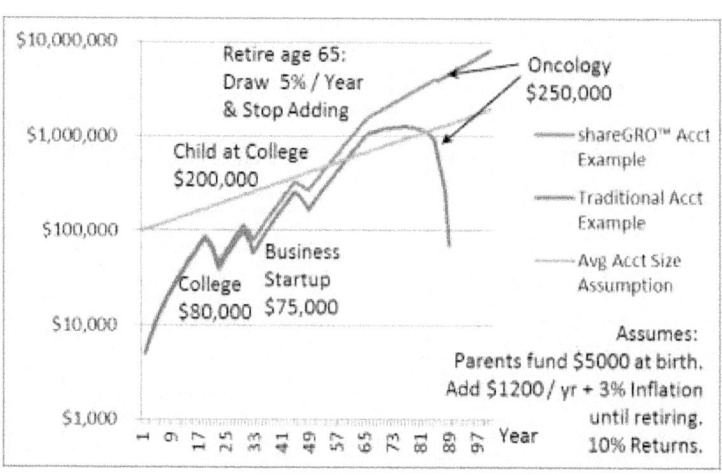

What it shows, is the comparison of an example set of scenarios in life with financial challenges, in this case, paying college expenses as a young adult, startup business expenses, putting a child through college, etc. including discontinuing paying into the investment account at retirement.

Suffice it that sharing can prevent running out of money, and help build a legacy to live on, and pass on. We can build something substantial, or provide a great start for the next generation. Perhaps that is the question. Would this help most people? The miracle is that this tiny 10 basis points of sharing that nobody will miss can help getting through college, business startup, putting kids through college, healthcare expenses, leaving "twelve basketsful" left over of legacy to heirs following a lifetime lived joyfully in liberty making the choices we want, not selections made for us. Oh, and leave an American dream (or emerging market person) dream intact for the next generation. This derives from integrating a portfolio of risk management, sharing and gleaning service, after God's design. And not requiring large paperwork for either private or government insurance scheme or scam.

Simple. Easy. Liberating. Like five loaves and two fish maybe.

Shall we give it a whirl?

www.StockRoller.com

REFERENCES

[i] http://www.rogerknapp.com/inspire/pickle_ja.htm
[ii] http://libertarianchristians.com/cfl/
[iii]
http://www.asanet.org/press/participation_in_voluntary_organizations_declining.cfm
[iv] https://www.stlouisfed.org/education/economic-lowdown-podcast-series/episode-2-factors-of-production
[v] https://en.wikipedia.org/wiki/Factors_of_production
[vi] http://smallbusiness.chron.com/economic-definition-four-factors-production-3941.html
[vii] Thomas Piketty, *Capital in the Twenty-First Century*, Pages 298 and 315.
[viii] http://www.usdebtclock.org/
[ix] https://www.cia.gov/library/publications/resources/the-world-factbook/geos/us.html
[x] https://en.wikipedia.org/wiki/George_III_of_the_United_Kingdom
[xi] https://en.wikipedia.org/wiki/The_Renaissance
[xii] https://en.wikipedia.org/wiki/Age_of_Enlightenment
[xiii] http://www.gutenberg.org/ebooks/816?msg=welcome_stranger
[xiv] https://vimeo.com/25741586
[xv] https://www.cia.gov/library/publications/the-world-factbook/geos/kn.html
[xvi] https://www.cia.gov/library/publications/the-world-factbook/geos/ks.html
[xvii] http://earthobservatory.nasa.gov/IOTD/view.php?id=83182
[xviii] https://en.wikipedia.org/wiki/Maisir
[xix] https://en.wikipedia.org/wiki/Sadaqah
[xx] https://en.wikipedia.org/wiki/Apologetics
[xxi] https://bber.unm.edu/econ/us-pci.htm
[xxii]
https://en.wikipedia.org/wiki/List_of_countries_by_wealth_per_adult
[xxiii] http://www.zerohedge.com/news/2013-06-02/its-1-world-who-owns-what-223-trillion-global-wealth
[xxiv] http://www.zerohedge.com/news/2013-06-02/its-1-world-who-owns-what-223-trillion-global-wealth
[xxv] http://cfk.unc.edu/aboutus/founders/
[xxvi] *Declaracion de Droits de l'homme* (1793), article 25

[xxvii] https://revnealvick.wordpress.com/2013/01/29/john-wesleys-3-general-rules/

[xxviii] http://www.povertyinc.org/

[xxix] http://www.povertyinc.org/

[xxx] https://en.wikipedia.org/wiki/Muhammad_Yunus

[xxxi] https://en.wikipedia.org/wiki/Grameen_Bank

[xxxii] http://www.ncrel.org/sdrs/areas/issues/students/atrisk/at6lk11.htm

[xxxiii] *Folklore of Finance* by Suzanne L. Duncan; Sean D. Fullerton, CFA; Samuel Humbert; Mirtha D. Kastrapeli; Kelly J. McKenna; and Nidhi V. Shandilya, CFA, sponsored by State Street, Center for Applied Research http://www.statestreet.com/content/dam/statestreet/documents/Articles/CAR/FolkloreofFinance_report.pdf

[xxxiv] http://www.intel.com/content/www/us/en/history/history-robert-noyce-man-behind-microchip-video.html